Greta
The Great Horned Owl

A True Story of Rescue and Rehabilitation

by Christie Gove-Berg

Adventure Publications
Cambridge, Minnesota

"For in the end, we will conserve only what we love. We will love only what we understand. We will understand only what we are taught." —Baba Dioum

Acknowledgments

Thank you to raptor centers and wildlife rehab centers; the work you do is vital, and I hope this book helps to further your efforts to educate and preserve. Special thanks to Amanda Nicholson, Dr. Peach Van Wick, and The Wildlife Center of Virginia for your expertise, photos, and the true story of this Great Horned Owl. Thank you to Dana and Rodney Lusher with Nature's Nanny Wildlife Rehabilitation; you rescued Greta from the train station, did her initial assessment, and transferred her to The Wildlife Center of Virginia; Greta may not have survived without your interventions and good local care. Thanks to Karla Bloem at the International Owl Center in Houston, Minnesota, for your support and for your mission to make the world a better place for owls through education and research. Thank you to The Raptor Center at the University of Minnesota for your support of my first raptor rescue story, *Esther the Eaglet*. And a huge thanks to the talented and generous photographers who donated their work so this story could be told: Dana and Rodney Lusher (Nature's Nanny), Peggy Naylor (Wildwoods), and Amanda Nicholson and The Wildlife Center of Virginia.

Photo credits by photographer and page number.

All images copyright of their respective photographers.

Front cover: Shutterstock.com: Imran Ashraf (flying owl); Curly Pat (background pattern); SagePhotography111 (main)

Back cover: Wildlife Center of Virginia (owl, woman); Shutterstock.com: Curly Pat (background pattern)

Rhoda Gerig: 11 (body), 27 (main owl); Peter L. Gove: 32; Shelly Hokanson: 23, 27 (release); Rodney Lusher: 12 (owl), 19 (crate: head), 20, 28; Stan Tekiela: 30 (feather); Wildlife Center of Virginia: 11 (head), 14–18, 19 (X-ray), 19 (leg), 21, 22 (perch), 25 (tub), 26 (woman), 31; Wildwoods: 19 (crate: body)

Shutterstock.com: Boy_Folio: 13 (rail yard); Alessandro Cancian: 6 (owl); ANGHI: 12 (tracks); Fall-line Photography: 22 (flying owl); John Gomez: 13 (man); Carol Gray: 24 (flying owl); IrinaK: 25 (mouse: bottom); ivgroznii: 6 (background pattern); Eric Isselee: 25 (mouse: top); kontur-vid: 7 (mouse); Curly Pat: background patterns (e.g. 4, 10, 13, 14, 16, 19, 20, 24, 26, 28); Scott David Patterson: 11 (train); picturepartners: 30 (pellet); Somkiet Poomsiripaiboon: 26 (glove); Ondrej Prosicky: 8 (fox); Patrick Rolands: 29 (owl, eye: wink); sasha2538: 8 (background pattern); torook: 25 (mouse: middle); VMCgroup: 8 (train); ZB2: 22 (background pattern); Milan Zygmunt: 4 (flying owl)

Edited by Ryan Jacobson

Cover and book design by Jonathan Norberg

Greta The Great Horned Owl

Greta
The Great Horned Owl

A True Story of Rescue and Rehabilitation

Greta the Great Horned Owl glides low over a field of grass. She listens for prey while her yellow eyes scan the landscape.

Greta's favorite time to hunt is at twilight. The sunset gives everything a warm glow. Night is coming.

A soft breeze blows across the field. Greta sees a small field mouse nibbling the seeds from a stalk of grass. Greta flies with silent wing strokes toward her prey.

She is hungry. She doesn't hear the low chug-chug of an engine or the loud thrum-thrum of wheels on metal.

Deer bound away, and foxes scurry out of sight. But Greta glides forward, low and fast. With her eyes and ears fixed on the mouse, she has no idea what is coming.

BAM!

The train hits Greta and pushes her forward. She is moving with the train.

Her legs and wings are trapped. She struggles but cannot get free. She is stuck against the front of the train.

The chug-chug sound slows and then stops. The train is no longer moving. Greta is in a dark, quiet building. She pulls and tugs her wing and legs. She frees herself from the train and falls to the floor.

When she tries to stand, her leg cannot hold her. Her wing hurts and she cannot fly. She sits on the hard ground as people watch. She is afraid.

Finally, a woman comes to help. She carefully lifts Greta off the floor and places her in a box. Greta feels so tired.

She is taken to a building where people examine her. They stretch out her wings and legs for pictures. They touch and poke her, but they are gentle.

Greta is moved to another location where a veterinarian can help her.

The vet finds that Greta has lost blood from a broken leg. Greta's right wing is broken too.

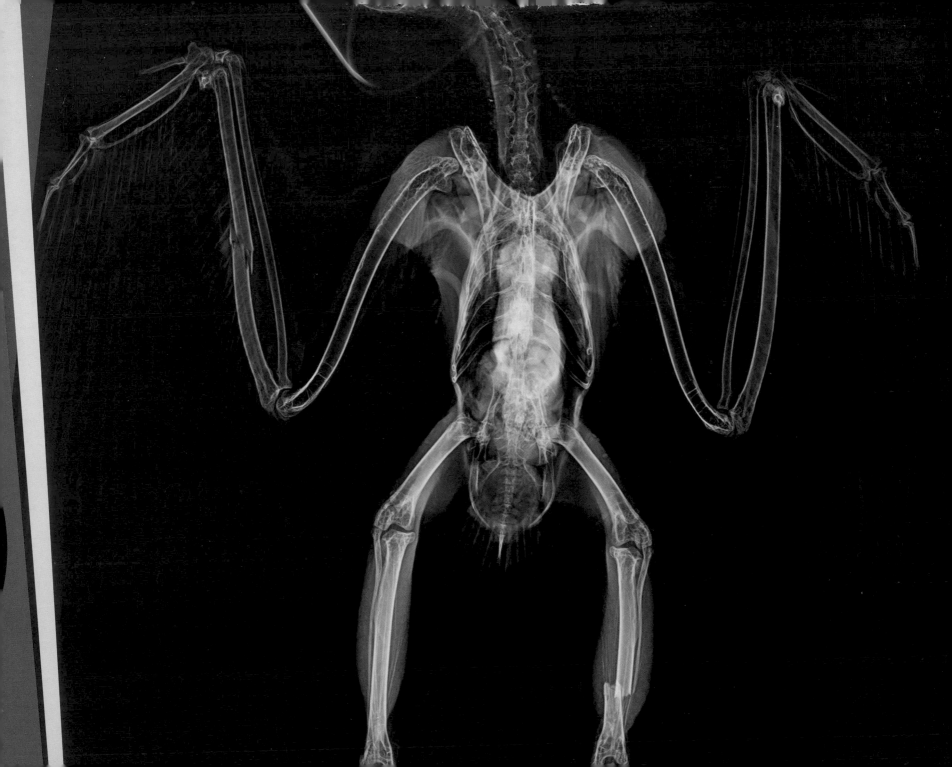

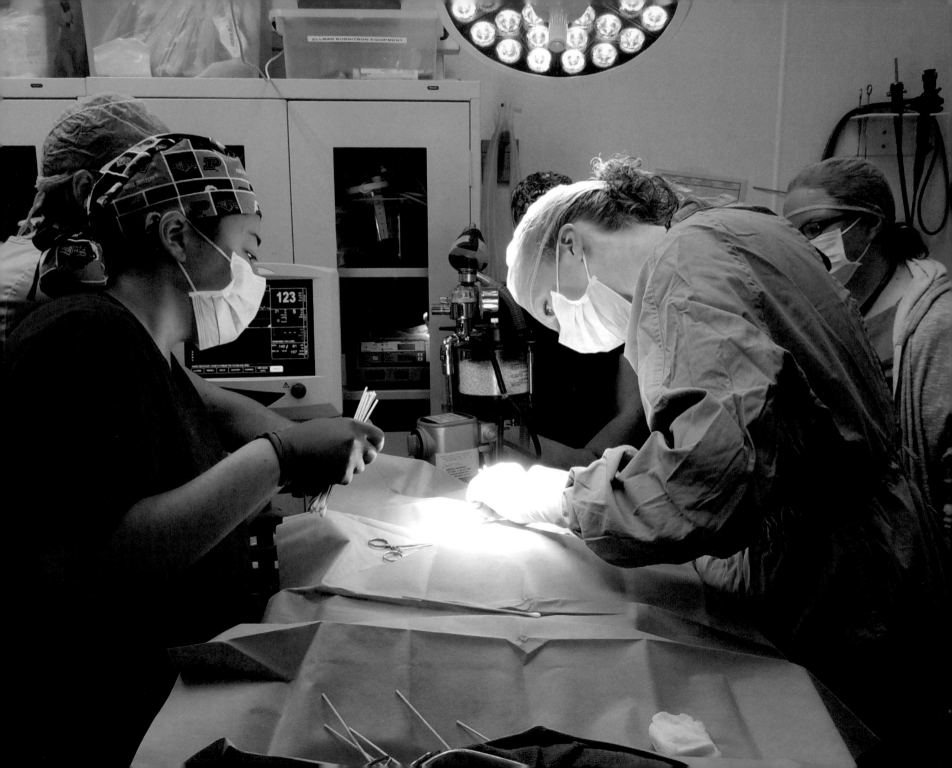

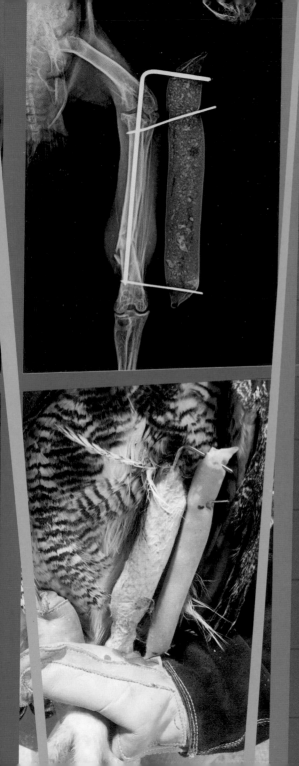

The vet gives Greta a shot and has her breathe special air that makes her sleepy. Then the vet works to fix the injuries.

Greta wakes to find a metal bar on her leg and a tight cloth wrapped around her wing. She cannot move her leg or her wing, but they hurt less.

For the next few days, Greta rests. She sleeps and eats in a small crate.

After a few weeks, the vet removes the bar from her leg and the wrapping from her wing. Workers move Greta outside. The warm sun and the cool wind feel so good.

Greta tries to open her right wing. It won't stretch out. It feels wrong.

"The wing has a patagial knot," says the veterinarian. "This is an area of tightness. It can happen when a wing is not moved for a long time."

Every day, the vet rubs the knot and stretches Greta's wing wide open.

The wing gets better, and Greta is moved into a large pen. She flies from end to end. It feels wonderful!

A large container is brought into her flight pen. It is filled with live mice. They rustle and scamper inside the container. Until now, the people have been feeding Greta dead mice. Greta's eyes focus and her talons twitch. She wants to hunt!

At twilight, she takes off from her spot in the flight pen. Swooping low, she grabs a mouse. Delicious!

The next day, the vet sees that Greta has eaten. She yells a happy, "Hooray!"

Greta is placed in a crate and gets a bumpy ride in the back of a car.

The vet removes her from the crate. Greta's large eyes take in a wide green field and tall trees. Her heart begins to race.

People watch and whisper as the vet throws Greta into the air.

Greta flies up toward the sky. The people cheer!

Greta lands on a tree branch at the edge of the field. It is nearly twilight, and Greta the Great Horned Owl is on the hunt again.

Why did Greta get hit by the train?

When owls, or other raptors, focus on their prey, they do not notice what is going on around them. It is likely that Greta didn't see the train and didn't hear its noise. The most common Great Horned Owl injury is being hit by a car. If you find an injured owl on the road, your family should call a wildlife rehabilitator.

What are raptors?

Raptors are meat-eating birds. They have hooked beaks, feet with sharp claws or talons, and good eyesight. Owls are a kind of raptor.

How do owls differ from other raptors, like hawks and eagles?

Most owls are nocturnal. They are awake at night and sleep during the day. Owls are the only nocturnal raptors, so they have amazing eyesight, even at night. They cannot move their eyes, though. Instead, they turn their heads to see to the side and behind their body.

Most owls fly more quietly than eagles and hawks. Their flight feathers have special edges that make them almost silent. Owls also have fluff on their feet and wings which absorb sound. Owls need to fly silently to surprise their prey.

Owls have excellent hearing. Their ears are on the sides of their face. When owls fly, their feathers help to push sound into their ears.

flight feather's special edge

What do Great Horned Owls eat?

Great Horned Owls eat almost anything. Most often, they eat smaller mammals or birds, but sometimes they eat other raptors or reptiles, insects, or fish. They even eat skunks. How? Owls don't really have a sense of smell, so skunk odor doesn't bother them!

They hunt at twilight, at night, and, sometimes, during the day. When they catch prey, they squeeze it with their strong talons. Great Horned Owls swallow small prey whole. They tear larger prey into pieces to swallow.

Does that mean they eat animal bones and fur, too?

Yes, they eat animal bones and fur, but they don't digest them. The bones, fur, and teeth form into pellets inside an owl's gizzard, which is its second stomach. Owls "cast" (cough up) about one pellet per day.

Where do Great Horned Owls live?

Great Horned Owls can be found in nearly all of North America and Central America. They have the largest range of any owl in North and Central America.

owl pellet

Tell me about their nests.

Great Horned Owls typically nest in trees. They might use a nest that was built by another bird. Or they might use a cavity (or hole) in a live tree, an empty building, a cave, or a cliff ledge. They sometimes nest on the ground.

Nests frequently fall apart over the breeding season, so it is normal for Great Horned Owls to find new nests every year.

Tell me about their families.

Great Horned Owls are monogamous. This means they stay with the same mate every year. The female is larger than the male and commonly lays 2 or 3 eggs. She incubates (sits on) the eggs to keep them warm. The eggs hatch in about a month. Both parents help to feed the baby owls, or owlets. It only takes 2 months for the owlets to learn to fly and leave the nest.

Great Horned Owls strongly defend their area. If there is a threat, they will hoot loudly, hiss, scream, and attack with wings and talons.

How will I know if an owl is a Great Horned Owl?

The male Great Horned Owl's call is the famous deep and loud, "Hoo, ho-hoo, hoo, hoo."

They have a barrel-shaped body, large head, and short wings. They are usually gray-brown in color with a reddish-brown face and a white patch on their throat, but their colors can vary quite a bit across their range.

On their heads, they have two "horns," which are actually feathers called plumicorns. Biologists aren't sure why Great Horned Owls have plumicorns. Some experts think they help them to camouflage, or hide. Some think plumicorns help them to attract a mate.

The plumicorn mystery remains to be solved. Maybe you will be the scientist who figures it out!

Why do they hoot?

Owls hoot mostly to talk with their mates or to mark their territory.

How long do owls live?

It is hard to know how long owls live. If they survive their first year, scientists believe they are capable of living into their teens, and a few make it into their 20s.

owlet

Tell me about wildlife rehabilitation centers.

Wildlife rehabilitation centers are places that treat injured animals. Some are small, local rehabilitation teams. They care for slightly injured or orphaned animals in their homes or at a small facility. Others are more like rehabilitation hospitals. There are veterinarians on site who are trained to take care of more serious injuries.

Tell me more about Greta.

Greta was picked up by a local team. When they found that her leg was broken, they sent her to a wildlife rehabilitation hospital. There, she was able to get pain medicine and the surgery that she needed. She also received long-term therapy for her wing. Thanks to both wildlife rehabilitation centers, Greta was able to return to the wild.

How did the wildlife rehabilitation center know that Greta could be let go?

The most important thing is whether or not an animal can feed itself. Owls need good ears, good eyes, and silent flight to hunt. In her flight pen, Greta proved that she could catch mice. So the team knew that she could survive in the wild.

How can I help to protect Great Horned Owls and other raptors?

Try to keep natural spaces open and wild. Birds and other animals need places to live, hunt, and raise their young. When parks close or forests are chopped down, there is less space for animals to live.

Ask your family to consider leaving dead trees standing. They provide homes for owls and many other forest friends.

Ask your family not to use rat/mouse poison. These poisons kill rodents, but they can also hurt or kill raptors that eat poisoned rodents.

Ask your family to take down unused soccer nets and remove old barbed wire because owls can get stuck and injured by these.

If you find an injured owl, have your family call a wildlife rehabilitation center.

By buying this book, you are donating to The Wildlife Center of Virginia. Consider visiting your local raptor center or wildlife rehabilitation center and donating time or money to their worthy work!

About the Author

Christie Gove-Berg loves nature and wildlife. Her first book, *Esther the Eaglet*, was written after the rescue of an injured eaglet on her parents' land. Her second raptor book, *Maggie the One-Eyed Peregrine Falcon*, was inspired by a young Peregrine Falcon that was injured while learning to fly in the middle of a big city. That bird is now an educational bird at The Wildlife Center of Virginia. A portion of proceeds from Christie's books goes to The Raptor Center at the University of Minnesota and The Wildlife Center of Virginia. Christie's regional book, *Minnesota Must-See for Families*, encourages families to document their Minnesota adventures together.